W9-BXL-154

COLORADO
Colors of the Rocky Mountains

Photographs by
STEVE TOHARI

**SHETLAND PRESS** • Breckenridge, Colorado

©1998 SHETLAND PRESS

All Photographs ©Steve Tohari

Third Printing 2004

Design by Steve Tohari

Text by Steve Tohari

Photo Editing by Steve Tohari

Type by Martha Bird

Encouragement by Pam Demma

SHETLAND PRESS

P.O. Box 5347

Breckenridge, Colorado 80424

Printed in Hong Kong

ISBN 0-9657504-2-6

Cover Photo: Indian Paintbrush, Engineer Pass near Silverton

PREFACE

I love Colorado.

After 15 years, I'm still looking for that "next picture". I look at a ridge high above and wonder what beautiful scene lies beyond it.

The colors of the Rocky Mountains are all beyond that ridge - so with my camera in my pack, I hike, climb, or ski to capture them on film.

Look at the pictures in this book and visualize yourself in a certain place at a certain time of the year, high in the Colorado Rockies.

Colorado is not just a beautiful place, but an *attitude* - a feeling of serenity and a belief that all can be right in this world.

STEVE TOHARI / Photographer - Photo Lab Technician   26 May 1998 - Breckenridge, Colorado

Aspen - Bighorn Creek above Vail

In early June, the Aspen leaf out and take on an emerald color that darkens as the summer progresses.

Aspen above McClure Pass

In the Elk Range south of Carbondale, Aspen leaves, blown by the wind, fall on an old logging road.

Morning after a big storm - Monarch Ski Area

Windblown snow at Monarch Pass flocks the trees at treeline on the southern end of the Sawatch Range near Salida.

Columbine - Yankee Boy Basin
above Ouray/San Juan Mountains

Colorado's state flower, Columbine, blooms in a high mountain basin above the town of Ouray (pronounced yoo-rey), named after a 19th century Indian Chief.

Aspen at Beaver Lake, Cimarron Creek
near Gunnison

Backlit Aspen leaves frame the volcanic Uncompahgre Range with a fence made of Aspen trees.

Peak 10 from Peak 8 - Breckenridge Ski Area

Fresh powder awaits adventurous skiers and snowboarders on a ridge at treeline south of Four O'clock Run.

Wildflowers at Lake Dillon

In early June, a south-facing slope is covered with wildflowers as snow melts on the Ten Mile Range.

Trail to Crater Lake from Maroon Lake, above Aspen

A hazy day in late September shows the yellow Aspen leaves at their peak - in a few days, the trees will be bare.

Union Bowl from Indian Ridge, Copper Mountain Ski Area

With ice-cream cone trees in the foreground, the jagged Ten Mile Range looms in the distance.

Indian Paintbrush - Governor Basin
above Ouray

A volcanic ridge, eroded into pinnacles, rises above a tundra dotted with wildflowers at over 13,000' elevation.

Dallas Divide - Autumn colors near Ridgway

From the divide, the San Juan Mountains rise in the distance, with yellow Aspen and rust-colored Oak covering the foothills.

Red Fox above Lake Dillon

Minutes after the sun had set behind the Ten Mile Range, a young fox came out of his den beneath the granite boulders, preparing to forage for his dinner.

Aspen - Ten Mile Range near Breckenridge

In an Autumn without snow, Aspen turn a brilliant gold above the glistening waters of Goose Pasture Tarn.

Snowstorm - Bear Creek near Evergreen

In early October, at 7,000' elevation, winter will soon cover this creek with snow and ice.

Wildflowers above Breckenridge

At over 11,000 feet, wildflowers finally bloom in mid-August for a brief period of two weeks before the snows of September.

Sunset - San Juan Mountains

The purple colors of sunset are reflected in a shallow pond below Dallas Divide near Ridgway.

Maroon Bells reflected in Maroon Lake, above Aspen

At the very end of September, the first snows have arrived, the Aspen have peaked, and leaves are falling.

North Peak at Keystone Ski Area

The formidable ski runs of North Peak are seen covered in a foot of fresh powder on a cloudy, windless day.

Pacific Peak, wildflowers above Breckenridge

Aster and two types of Indian Paintbrush grow at the edge of a tarn - a shallow pond - above Mohawk Lakes in the Ten Mile Range.

Old barn near Lake City

Cottonwoods are reflected in a small pond in the northern reaches of the San Juan Range south of Gunnison.

Bighorn Sheep on Trail Ridge, Rocky Mountain National Park

In early June, at over 12,000' elevation, an old ram poses by the highest continuous paved road in America.

Sunset reflections near Twin Lake

On the winding road to Independence Pass, on the way to Aspen, the massive 14,000' peaks of the Elk Range catch the last golden rays of the sun.

Mt. Wilson, San Miguel Mountains
near Telluride

Old-growth Aspen in brilliant Autumn color are seen from Sunshine Campground on the way to Lizardhead Pass.

Fog - Aspen Ski Area

In a light snowstorm at the top of Aspen Mountain, a heavy fog shrouds a lone tree in soft shades of black and white.

Maroon Bells above Maroon Lake - near Aspen

The reddish sediments from the eroding Maroon Bells take on purple and turquoise colors as winds rake across Maroon Lake in mid-June.

Wildflowers - Yankee Boy Basin above Ouray

Indian Paintbrush, Bluebells, Wildrose, and Columbine grow below the shrinking snows of the San Juan Mountains in late July.

Back Bowls of Vail - Vail Ski Area

Replenished with more deep snows from a recent storm, the expansive bowl-shaped terrain behind Vail Mountain is a paradise in blue.

Headwaters of Swan River, above Breckenridge

Above treeline, just below the Continental Divide, Parry's Primrose grows on a wet stream bank.

Near Owl Creek Pass, Uncompahgre Range

Chimney Rock, a volcanic formation, towers above a meadow surrounded by Aspen shedding their leaves in early October.

Aspen reflections near Crystal City

The colors of early Autumn are reflected in a puddle on the Schofield Pass Road, a century-old mining road connecting the towns of Marble and Crested Butte in the Elk Range south of Aspen.

Wildflowers above Silverton